T0128723

Collections of Love

Loves & Pains of Kesha Laine, VOL. 1

A volume of poetry written from 1973 to 2016

Karen E. Scowden

AKA: Kesha Laine

authorHOUSE®

AuthorHouse™
1663 Liberty Drive
Bloomington, IN 47403
www.authorhouse.com
Phone: 1 (800) 839-8640

Published by AuthorHouse   04/22/2016

ISBN: 978-1-5246-0409-7 (sc)
ISBN: 978-1-5246-0407-3 (hc)
ISBN: 978-1-5246-0408-0 (e)

Library of Congress Control Number: 2016906233

Print information available on the last page.

This edition involves the heartbreak of love, lost love, and the Never ending hope for finding love.

Beginning......

The yard swings' paint is peeling.
The grass has begun to turn brown.
Oh, how I love this feeling?
This blue, melancholy down.
The leaves are slowly turning,
And beginning to fall to the ground.
The fire for you that was burning,
Like the leaves, is falling down.
The summer days are about over,
And the sun doesn't shine so long.
So I say goodbye to my lover,
And silently walk on home.

KL: August 1967

One sunny afternoon,
When I had nothing else to do
I sat myself down and thought,
Well, I'd better write my love a letter
I'd write it long, I'd write it neat
I'd start it with "Darling:"
And end it with, "I love you, but; I am sorry."
I'd stick to the subject, Not go into the past
Yes, I would have to write it good
Because it would be my last.
I started to begin.
But had to stop and think:
What was that crystal clear thing?
Running down my cheek?
Yes, it was a tear.
Followed by another.
I then looked across the pier,
And saw that it was raining.

The sun had gone behind a cloud.

The birds went to their nest.

The sky had turned gray

And everything began to fade away

I seemed to go into a trance,

I heard a familiar voice

Come from out of the past

And then I saw:

A tear stained letter

In my own handwriting

My very own words

Then I saw a boy crying.

The boy I knew.

Yes, it was him.

But why?

But how?

But when?

KEH/KL/10/31/1967

TO YOU

How can I tell you?
Or even begin to write
Of the things I've thought of
Every day and night
Since you left me,
Walked out that door,
Into the night.
And the reasons for
You leaving me-
Alone.
With a feeling
I had never known.
Before ....
this happened-
We were happy!
Or had been
Until she came
Into your life.
Now it isn't the same
Without you-
To love me
Or care. You see:
Loneliness I just can't bear

1971///KES

FEELINGS

The night is cold and lonely
The wind is very still
I lie upon my bed-alone-
Trying not to feel:
The loneliness
And pain
The sadness from adventures
That never came.
Was it yesterday?
Or the day before?
That he left me,
For adventures off the shore.
Days have come and gone.
Still no word have I.
God! Where can he be?
Is he still alive?!
Although he does not know,
His baby inside me grows.
But for what purpose?
For what reason, I do not know.

KES/KL: August 1971/March 1972

Everything is Hazy

Everything is hazy
So dark and cold.
I think I am going crazy.
I feel so alone.
I can't sleep at nights
For fear you will call
What gives you the right?
It should be against the law!
Everything is hazy
I can't feel a thing
I think I'm going crazy
Oh, how can I sing?
I feel so lonely
Since you went away
Oh, God, how can I live
Through one more day?
Everything is hazy
So dark and so cold.
I think I'm going crazy
I feel so alone.

KES/KL: Sept. 1971

QUIET WINDS

Quite winds
Whispering thru the night
What are you trying to tell me?
Please,
Come nearer
So I can hear you.
Stop!
Don't pass me by.
I am so lonely here
Just talk to me a while
What?
I didn't understand.
Quiet winds,
Whispering thru the night,
Don't desert me.
Don't leave me here alone.

KES

YOUTH

Eyes so blue
And kind.
A young and
Innocent mind.
Mouth,
So quick to smile
Come,
Talk to me awhile.
Lips,
Trembling with fear-
Ears,
So willing to hear.
A soul
That's good
And free-
I would love you IF I could……

KES/KL: July 1973

NO MAN

No man to cling to
No man to hold me tight
No man to reach out for
On these long and cold lonely nights
No man to cuddle up to
No man to whisper soft love into
My ear
No man to protect me
No man always near.
No man to hug me.
No man to kiss away these tears.
No man to soothe me, or.
Take away my fears.
No man to love me.
No man to want me.
No man to need me.
No man.
No, Not since you.

KES/KL: April 1971

HIM

He is gone.
He left me.
I don't even know where he went.
I don't even know why:
Or care!
Not anymore:
Not after the way he treated me.
NO!
I'm not worried.
I don't need him.
Or want him.
He is nothing to me.
When he was here,
All he did was yell and scream
And hurt me.
He wasn't any good
I really didn't even love him.
Honest?
Didn't I?
Then, why am I crying?

KES/KL: April 1973

OF YOU

The warmth of your embrace
The firmness of your face.
The glint of your eyes.
The softness of your sighs
The moistness of your lips
The tenderness of your kiss.
The lightness of your laugh
The brightness of your smile
The gentleness of your touch
I miss so very much.
The things you used to say
The kind and gentle way
The things you used to do
The love you gave too
The graceful way you used to move
The gentle way you used to love
All of these and so much more,
I miss. So, come back please.

Kes

EYES

Big,

Big brown

Big brown eyes.

Your eyes.

Seeing me for the very first time.

Seeing me as I really am.

Not was,

Or will be.

Just me…

And….

You see.

You see in me.

You see in my eyes.

You see you in my eyes-

From my eyes,

And, I know:

I love you.

I know,

You love me.

So, why can't it be?

kes

NEVER

I will never see another sunrise.
I will never hear the birds sing again.
I will never feel another fresh, spring rain.
I will never smell another field of clover.
And I will never take another lover.
Because, I cannot see.
Or feel
Or hear.
Or smell.
Because you left me,
And I am dead

may1973-kesha

WHEN

Here I am
So alone
And it is getting darker
I wish you'd come home.
I've missed you
So very much
All day
I have longed for your touch.
I start
at every passing car
And I've began to wonder
Where you are.
It's getting later
The night air is cool
But that doesn't matter
Because----When you come home
You'll put your arms

Around me
And make me warm.
And you'll laugh
At me
Because I've been crying
And you'll tell me
How silly it was to worry.
Yes, When you
Come home.
Everything will be fine
I won't be alone
When you come home.

/KL: June 13,1973

PASSING

The times he held me
Were not many
The times he kissed me
Were just as few.
He wasn't such a gentle man
Nor was he so very kind,
But every time he took me,
There wasn't a doubt in my mind.
He wasn't here so very long
Before he went away,
But I don't care what you say!
It was ME he loved, NOT you!!!

kes

HE

He came,
And stayed a while.
Just long enough
To make me smile
Just long enough
To teach me life
But not long enough
To make me his wife.
He taught me to laugh
And to sing.
He taught me
So very many things.
He gave me happiness
And tears.
He gave me sadness
And fears.
He gave to me.
He taught me.
He came to me.
And he left me.
But, most of all…...... He loved me
Didn't he?

kes/june 1973

REASON

Crystal clear droplets
Falling from the sky.
Oh, my darling,
What has happened to you and I?
What happened to all the good times
That we used to have?
What happened to the smiles
And the way we used to laugh?
How come now all we
Do is fight?
How come lately,
You've been coming home so late at night?
Why did you think I had
Betrayed you?
Why did you think I'd
Stopped being true?
Just because I don't say it,
Doesn't mean I don't love you.
Haven't you noticed the things
That I do?
The ways in which I try
To show you?
Just to prove how much
I love you?

KES/KL: May 1973

SUMMER STORMS--Part 1

Last night we had a fight.
And this morning, you left
Without kissing me good-bye.
All day I have worried.
Thought something terrible
might happen:
That you might die.
And you'd never know
Just how much I love you.
Or how much I care.
So tonight, just as soon as you
Walk through this door,
I'm gona tell you how sorry I am
About the night before.

kesha

Summer Storms Part 2.

Please hold me.
Protect me from the night.
Put your strong arms around me,
Hold me tight.
Protect me from this darkness
That is slowly creeping through the door.
Warm me from this coldness,
Before, I am no more.
Come, comfort me.
Tell me it's alright.
Tell me it's just the wind,
Blowing through the night.
Come, Kiss my forehead.
Make these bad thoughts go away!
Come to my bed.
Come to where I lay.
Tale me in your arms.
Soothe away the pain.

Let our one night together,
Be not in vain! Just hold me.
Keep me warm
Come, Protect me,
From this summer storm.
Be gentle, And kind....
Imprint upon my mind—
This one night.
Our little love affair.
You're just like the others! You don't even care!!!

kesha

VISION

The lingering of your scent behind you
As you leave,
Make me feel so sad inside.
So I take a deep breath.
And close my eyes.
And I see you once more--
Beside me, and you are crying too.
Deep inside, throbbing with unshed tears.
And you reach out to me.
And you take me in your arms.
You hold me, and kiss my lips.
I open my eyes.
And there you are.
Beside me.
And, you are crying too.

June 1973
KES/KL

GOODBYE

I close my eyes to you.
My hands touch the roughness
Of your face.
My fingers follow the arch
Of your brow.
They trace the fine featured nose,
And glide around to caress the ringlets
Of hair at your neck.
My lips brush across your forehead.
And I bless both of your eyes.
I kiss your lips,
And say Good-bye.
I close my heart to you.

July 1973KEsHA

DREAM

Night stranger, visiting my bed.
You are only a vision.
A shadow on the wall.
Night stranger, flashing through my mind
You are merely a fantasy.
My imagination, is all.
Night stranger, forever haunting me
Go away! Leave me alone!
Stop frightening me.
You are not real.
You are dead.

August 20, 1973
KES/KL

BLUE MORNING

Blue morning, so dull and gray.
It has been like this, since you went away.
Blue morning, always so cold.
I feel just awful,
So depressed and alone.
Blue morning,
Without you here,
Life just doesn't seem worth it.
It's a bit more than I can bear.
Blue morning, please give me a break!
Let the sun shine in,
Before it's too late.

Sept. 1973
KES/KL

IF YOU LOVE ME

From the east comes the sun.
And with it, comes a deep loneliness
That has been hidden within myself-
Since that day you left.
You came into my life suddenly,
Yet, knowingly.
I stopped by and watched
With depressing eyes. -
As your love slowly died.
I didn't stop or tardy your stay.
Although I wanted to.
Your life gave me warmth.
Your arms gave me strength.
Your eyes shone with pride
Of being who you were.
You climbed the height of the sky-
And beamed down upon me,
Your love-giving smile.

On you climbed across the Heavens.
At times you were weary,
And asked for comfort.
That I could not give.
I only felt a touch of your love.
Yet, it made me glow-
With a beautiful feeling
For it was better to have loved you
Than not to have felt your love at all.

KESHA

IF ONLY

Knowing the love and care-
You could have filled my life with.
And as your soft brown body,
Touched mine for the last time-
I felt the love from your body
Flowing to mine.
Never forgetting you are
Still a part of me.
The many times I've been alone,
And the many times I have cried:
Anyway, you will never know
The many times I've tried.
You left me standing here.
Don't keep me waiting.
Let me know the way,
Show me to your door.
Come back and say
The things you used to say.

As my memories turn back the pages

I can see, the happy times

We spent before.

Now the love that kept this heart beating-

Has been shattered

By the closing of the door

My world is cold and still.

My dreams lie unfulfilled.

I'll never stop believing: in the future:

We will love like we used to do…

kesha

I LOVE YOU

I am so sorry I did you wrong.
Please come and get me.
And take me to your world.
All I want, is to be your love, once more.
Please come back.
Kiss away the tears.
Make this heart worthwhile again.
Only you can change the blue days
Make them go away.
But, it's all over.
Except for the loneliness
That gets to me somehow.
My eyes would like to see you
Walk right through that door.
And into this lonely night.
But, I might as well admit it,
It's all over now.

Karen Elaine Holsinger/Scowden
Kesha Laine

October 22, 1971

SEASONS OF LIFE

THE WIND IS HOWLING THROUGH THE NOW NAKED TREES.
THERE AREN'T ANY LEAVES TO SOFTEN THE PIERCING
SHARPNESS OF THE NIGHT AIR.
THERE ISN'T A MOON TO LIGHTEN THE DARKNESS THAT
IS SO FRIGHTENING.
THE CLOUDS HAVE COVERED THE STARS AND THERE IS
NO LIFE UPON THIS EARTH.
ONLY STILLNESS AND THIS QUIET GLOOM THAT HAUNTS
THIS GOD FORESAKEN GARDEN
WHERE THERE ONCE WAS LIFE AND LAUGHTER, AND LOVE.
BUT, ALAS!! TIME PASSES AND ONE GROWS OLD.
BUT NOT SOON ENOUGH TO BE SPARED THE HELL ONE
MUST GO THROUGH
WHEN A LOVED ONE GOES AWAY.
TO A BETTER PLACE OR PERSON, HE THOUGHT MORE
BEAUTIFUL THAN ME!!
ONLY TO DISCOVER TOO LATE, THAT THE ONLY LOVE
THERE WAS, HAS GONE AWAY.
FOR WHEN HE FINALLY COMES BACK TO ME, THERE WILL
ONLY BE
THE FROST BITTEN ROSES OF SUMMER LEFT TO REMIND
HIM OF

THE LOVE WE SHARED BEFORE.
AND THE WIND WILL HOWL OVER THIS DARK DESERTED GARDEN,
WHERE THERE ISN'T ANY MOON OR STARS TO LIGHT HIS PATH.
BUT PERHAPS, HE WILL FEEL THIS LOVE FROM ABOVE, AND KNOW
THAT I AM STILL WAITING FOR HIM.

kesha

Seasons #2

I have waited through the spring and he did not call.

I walked through the long days of summer, still no word from him.

Fall came and passed without him. There was no answer.

Now that winter has come again, the pain is gone. I feel nothing.

Perhaps, when I see the fresh new green grass and flowers in the spring;

Something will stir inside me; Make me come to life. But now is just the winter.

So cold and barren. I still must suffer alone.

For while I feel nothing—He is happy with her.

KESHA /KL

ONLY WORDS

Love is just a word used by men as a weapon to get what they want.

It used to be a lovely word two people shared with happiness and pleasure

They found in each others presence.

But now, again: I find it is just a word misused for lust and mistaken for charm.

It is actually a pretty word for hate.

What else could it be? These bruises on my face are love?!

The screaming and shouting threats are love?

The attempts of suicide are love?

NO!!! My darling, this is not love. Not love at all!!!

KES/1973-1974

BLINDING RAIN

The rain hitting against the window pane, blinding me.
Freeing me from seeing my own tears
Lightning piercing the darkness of the sky like the pain that
Is searing through my heart.
Thunder roaring through the air, drowning out my fears.
The moon hidden by the clouds, peeps in and out like
A winking eye. looking down upon me.
While the wind whistles laughter through the forest,
Mocking me for the fool that I have been.

November 73/sept. 74
KEH/KES/KL

UNTIL TOMORROW

UNTIL TOMORROW, I WILL HOLD YOU IN MY ARMS
LET YOU TEASE ME WITH YOUR CHARMS.
I WILL LISTEN INTENTLY TO YOUR WORDS OF LOVE
I WILL LET YOU KISS ME,
I WILL GIVE YOU AN EXTRA HUG.
FOR PRETENDING THAT YOU NEED ME.
AND WANT ME ALWAYS WITH YOU
EVEN THOUGH YOU SEE
THE SEARCHING IN MY EYES FOR THE TRUTH,
INSTEAD OF LIES.
BUT I WILL LET YOU TAKE ME, KNOWING THIS
IS THE WAY IT HAS TO BE.
SO COME! KISS AWAY THE SORROW,
AND I WILL BE WITH YOU UNTIL TOMORROW…

kes/1975

PLEA OF MERCY

PLEASE, DON'T CAUSE ME ANY MORE PAIN!
I'VE HAD ENOUGH!
JUST LOOK AT THE BED WHERE I'VE LAIN.
SEE THE CRUMPLED SHEETS?
THE BATTERED PILLOWS?
SEE THE FADED BLOOD STAINS?

PLEASE, DON'T HARM ME!
DON'T HURT ME AGAIN!

PLEASE!

August 1974
Karen Holsinger/kesha laine.

DAWN

THE SUN IS RISING AGAIN,

WITHOUT YOU.

I SLEPT THROUGH THE NIGHT,

NOT LONGING FOR YOU.

BUT THE MOON, CAUGHT ME PEEPING.

LOOKING FOR YOU

AND THE STARS SAW ME CRYING:

BUT NOT OVER YOU.

July 5, 1973
Karen Holsinger/kesha laine

WISHES

OH, MY DARLING, PLEASE LINGER.

JUST A FEW MORE MINUTES LONGER.

HOLD ME IN YOUR ARMS AGAIN.

LET THINGS BE AS THE WERE.

FOR WHEN YOU ARE BESIDE ME,

YOUR WARMTH FLOWS THROUGH MY SKIN.

AND THERE IS NOTHING TO REMIND ME

OF LONG AGO COMMITED SINS.

I KNOW, DARLING, THAT YOU TOLD ME:

WHERE THERE IS LOVE, THERE IS NO SIN.

BUT I STILL CAN'T HELP WISHING

THAT IT WERE YOU WHO TOOK ME, NOT HIM.

Kesha Laine

BLAME

HOW CAN I EVER FORGET YOU?

OR PUT YOU OUT OF MY MIND?

AND NOT SEE YOUR FACE

FLASHING THROUGH MY MIND?

HOW CAN I FORGIVE YOU?

FOR THE HELL YOU PUT ME THROUGH?

FOR ALL THE PAIN IV'E SUFFERED,

I BLAME MYSELF, NOT YOU.

FOR I WAS THE ONE WHO GAVE IN.

I WAS THE ONE WHO MADE THE MISTAKE.

IT IS I WHO COMMITED THE SIN.

1973
KAREN HOLSINGER/KESHA LAINE

AM I BAD?

I GAVE MYSELF TO HIM
BECAUSE I LOVED HIM
AND HE LOVED ME.
AND I DIDN'T WANT TO LOOSE HIM.
BUT I LOST HIM ANYWAY.

AM I BAD?

I WAS LONELY.
SO I GAVE MYSELF TO YOU:
BUT YOU WENT AWAY TOO.

AM I BAD?

I AM HUNGRY FOR A MAN.
SOMEONE TO GIVE MY LOVE TO.
HOW ABOUT YOU?

AM I BAD?

Kesha

THIS IS WHY

BEING THERE WHEN I WANT YOU.
BEING THERE WHEN I REACH OUT
BEING THERE TO HOLD ME
DIMINISHING ALL MY DOUBTS.

SHARING WITH EACH OTHER
ALL THE THIGS WE'VE HAD
GIVING LIFE TO ONE ANOTHER.
BEING HAPPY AND NOT SAD.

TRUSTING EACH OTHER
WITH EVERYTHING WE OWN.
STAYING TOGETHER
NEVER LEAVING ME ALONE.

THIS IS WHY I LOVE YOU.
WITH ALL MY HEART AND SOUL.
AND WHY I'LL NEVER LEAVE YOU
NEVER, MY DARLING, NO.

AUGUST 1973.
KAREN HOLSINGER/KESHA LAINE

RED VELVET

RED VELVET ON MY PILLOW.

RED VELVET ON MY BED

LISTENING TO THE RADIO

TO WHAT THE DISC JOCKEY SAID.

IT'S NOW 2:37AM

JUST LYING HERE

LISTENING TO HIM,

AND DRINKING ANOTHER BEER.

LOSING MYSELF IN THE MELODY.

TAPPING MY FOOT ON THE WALL.

UNRAVELING MY MIND, SETTING IT FREE

CLOSING MY EYES, THAT'S ALL……

july73/kes

SCARLET LADY

LADY IN RED, UPON THIS BED

SING ME A LITTLE SONG.

ABOUT THIS LIFE THAT YOU NOW LEAD.

TELL ME HOW YOU WENT WRONG.

July 1973
KAREN HOLSINGER/KESHA LAINE

FANTASY

COME,
TAKE ME BY THE HAND.
TAKE ME TO NEVER NEVER LAND.
WHERE PEOPLE ALWAYS
LAUGH AND SING.
WHERE THERE IS ONLY VERY
SIMPLE THINGS.
WHERE THERE IS LOVE
WITHOUT PAIN.
WHERE NO TEARS ARE SHED.
AND NO MEAN WORDS ARE SAID.
WHERE PEOPLE LIVE WITHOUT GUILT.
AND NO INSTITUTIONS ARE BUILT.
WHERE THE SUN ALWAYS SHINES
AND THERE ARE NO CRIMES.
WHERE SEX ISN'T A SIN.
THERE IS NO "OUT", AND NO "IN"
WHERE THE SKY IS ALWAYS BLUE
THERE IS ONLY ME AND YOU.
TO LIVE AND LEARN.
TO LAUGH AND LOVE
EACH OTHER.

kesha

THE END

THE LAST TIME I SAW HIM, WAS
WHEN WE SAID GOODNIGHT.
AND HE TOLD ME, THAT HE WOULD SEE
ME COME THE MORNING LIGHT.
HE PROMISED THAT HE'D BRING ME
SOMETHING TO MAKE ME SMILE
HE GENTLY LAUGHED AND KISSED ME.
AND TOLD ME HE'D BE BACK IN A LITTLE WHILE.
HE TOLD ME TO REMEMBER
ALWAYS, THAT HE LOVED ME TRUE
AND NEVER TO DOUBT HIS WORDS,
LEAST HE'D GO BACK TO YOU.
BUT, HE TAUGHT ME,
NOT TO BELIEVE EVERYTHING
PEOPLE SAID.
I KNOW HE ISN'T COMING BACK.
HE IS LIVING WITH YOU INSTEAD.

Kesha Laine

EX'ES

IT'S OVER NOW
I KNOW FOR SURE.
I DON'T KNOW HOW
I STOOD IT THIS LONG.
YOU TALK OF LOVE,
BUT ALL IS FEEL IS PAIN.
IT'S JUST A PHRASE
USED OVER AND OVER AGAIN.
YOU SAY YOU CARE,
BUT IT IS HARD TO BELIEVE
BY THE WAY YOU BEHAVE
WHEN YOU ARE WITH ME.
I DON'T LIKE THE PAIN,
I'M NO FIGHTER,
SO, INSTEAD OF YELLING:
JUST HOLD ME A BIT TIGHTER
I DON'T LIKE TO CRY
BUT IT HURTS SO BAD.
I'M TIRED OF ALL YOUR FUSSNG
I'M TIRED OF BEING SAD
THIS ISN'T LOVE,
THIS ISN'T A LIFE.
I WOULD RATHER LIVE ALONE FOREVER
THAN TO LIVE IN HELL AS YOUR WIFE!

kesha

SILENT MUSIC

MUSIC MAN, COME SING ME A SONG.

SING IT LOUD SO IT WILL DROWN OUT

THE ANGER AND HURT INSIDE OF ME.

BUT SING IT SOFTLY LIKE

SILENT MEMORIES WISPERING

THROUGH MY MIND.

SING IT FOREVER, SO I WON'T HAVE TO

REMEMBER THE PAIN OF LOVING YOU.

NO, STOP! IT'S ALREADY TOO LATE.

KAREN HOLSINGER/KESHALAINE.
1974

IV'E GOT THE BLUES

OH BABY, I'VE GOT THE BLUES FOR YOU!
I MISS YOU SO VERY MUCH.
I CLOSE MY EYES AND IMAGINE
YOUR WARM AND GENTLE TOUCH.
I THINK ABOUT CONSTANTLY,
AND MAKE BELIEVE YOU ARE NEAR.
DARLING, I NEED YOU SO VERY MUCH.
I WISH THAT YOU WERE HERE.
HONEY, I DREAM ABOUT YOU EVERY NIGHT.
AND BELIEVING THAT YOU ARE HERE,
I REACH OUT TO LOVE YOU
BUT YOU SIDE IS ALWAYS BARE.
I KNOW I MUST CALL YOUR NAME OUTLOUD
AS OFTEN AS I HAVE DREAMED OF YOU.
ANY MANY TIMES I HAVE WONDERED-
ARE YOU DOING THE SAME THING TOO?

DECEMBER 1974
KAREN HOLSINGER/KESHA LAINE.

LIMBO

FOR MANY MILES I HAVE WALKED ALONE
CRYING IN THE NIGHT
AND MANY TIMES I'VE BEEN COLD
FROM HAVING NO WHERE TO GO
I HAVE WAKENED IN MORNINGS
THAT I THOUGHT I WOULD NEVER SEE.
AND BEEN KISSED BY MEN
THAT I WOULD NEVER KNOW.
I HAVE DREAMED, HOPED, AND PRAYED
FOR SOME MAN TO LOVE ME BACK.
I THOUGHT I'D FINALLY FOUND ONE.
BUT WE ARE SO FAR APART.
I WANT YOU TO KNOW, I LOVE YOU,
MORE THAN EVER BEFORE.
BUT YOU ARE SO FAR AWAY,
AND I AM ALL ALONE.
AND I NEED SOMEONE TO STAY.

November 1975
Karen Holsinger/kesha laine.

Empty Corners

Empty corners and memories
Etched upon my mind
I wish I could forget
But I know I'll always find:
Sneaking around the corners
Peeping through someway
Those wretched little memories
I wish would go away.
Sometimes I find something
I wish we could have shared,
But I always find myself glad
Of the pain that you were spared.
Those awful, horrid memories
Running through my head
Often make me wish
That I was sometimes dead.
Those dreadful thoughts
Always dashing all around,
Can really make a person:
A body, feel so down.
Such morbid remembrances
For someone so young.

I often times wonder
Just what it is I've done?
Such bittersweet memories
Of days so long ago
Finally, all washed away ....
By a man I now know.

kesha

FEAR

THERE IS FEAR, SLOWLY RISING UP IN MY SOUL.
CHOKING MY HEART, AND MAKING MY BELLY ACHE.
FEAR FROM STRANGERS WALKING PAST MY HOUSE.
FEAR FROM BEING ALONE TONIGHT.
FEAR THAT YOU WON'T CALL
AND FEAR FROM YOUR LEAVING ME IN THE FIRST PLACE-
ALWAYS FEAR-
AFRAID TO TOUCH
AND OF NOT BEING TOUCHED.
WHAT IS THIS CRAZY LIFE THAT WE HAVE TO LIVE?
THAT MAKES US SO AFRAID OF EACH OTHER?
WHEN ALL WE WANT TO DO IS:
REACH OUT-
AND TOUCH EACH OTHER.
BUT, WE ARE ALL SO AFRAID
I SEE YOU LOOKING AT ME.
AND THERE IS FEAR SLOWLY RISING UP IN MY SOUL;
CHOKING MY HEART, AND MAKING MY BELLY ACHE.

April 1975/Kesha

THE INVADER

HE COMES INTO MY LIFE
LIKE A CAT
QUIETLY STALKING
IN THE NIGHT.

HE SITS AND WAITS
READY TO POUNCE
WHEN I AM UNPREPARED
AND IT IS TOO LATE.

TO PROTECT MYSELF
FROM HIS SOFT WORDS
AND HIS GENTLE CARRESSES
AND HE KNOWS I AM AFRAID.

AFRAID TO RUN
FROM HIM
AND I CAN'T QUITE BRING MYSELF
TO HIM.

BECAUSE IT WILL
ALL BE OVER
WHEN I DO GIVE IN
A ND HE WILL GO----------- AND I WILL BE ALONE AGAIN.

Aug.1975

BROKEN DREAMS

BROKEN DREAMS AND PROMISES
WISHES UNFULLFILLED
REMEMBERING ALL THE PLANS WE HAD
THE HOUSE WE WERE GOING TO BUILD.

MEMORIES OF A BITTER PAST
THE YEARS SO LONG AGO
STILL MARRED UPON MY MIND
THE HURT NO ONE KNOWS.

TEARS FALLING DOWN MY CHEEK
FAINT WHISPERS OF THE WORDS:
"DARLING, WE SHALL NEVER PART"

ECHOING THROUGH THE HOLLOW CHAMBERS
AND TUMBLING BACK TO MY MIND.
RAMBLING AROOUND WITH A BROKEN HEART
NO PEACE ON EARTH SHALL I FIND.

OH, LORD! COME TAKE THIS PAIN AWAY!
MELT THIS FEAR WITHIN
FORGIVE ME FOR NEGLECTING YOU.
GOD, PLEASE FORGIVE ME FOR MY SINS.

Aug/75

IV'E BEEN A FOOL

I BEEN A FOOL, AGAIN.
I LET A MAN LOVE ME;
WITHOUT LOVING ME.
HE TOOK ME IN HIS ARMS
TO COMFORT ME
HE HELD ME CLOSE
THEN HE LET ME BE.
I'VE BEEN A FOOL, AGAIN.
I LET A MAN LOVE ME
WITHOUT LOVING ME
HE TOOK MY HAND
AND LED ME ON
HE WAS HERE LAST NIGHT
BUT NOW, HE'S GONE.
I'VE BEEN A FOOL, AGAIN.
I LET A MAN LOVE ME
WITHOUT LOVING ME.
HE HELD ME TIGHT.
AND TOLD ME LIES
THEN HE LEFT.
WITHOUT SAYING GOODBYS.
I'VE BEEN A FOOL, AGAIN.
I LET A MAN LOVE ME
WITHOUT LOVING ME

kesha

LIGHTNING STRICKS

THE BALMY BREEZE
AND CRISP, GREEN GRASS
FORSAKEN MEMORIES
FROM THE PAST.
THE BRIGHT BLUE SKY
AND THE WARM SUNSHINE
JUST YOU AND I
WITH LOVE ON OUR MINDS.
WALKING TOGETHER
PICKING FLOWERS
IT'LL BE FOREVER!
ONLY OURS!
THE SUDDEN RAIN
AND THE THUNDER STORMS
THE QUICK, SHARP PAIN-
THEN, NOTHING MORE.

May KESHA

EMPTY ARMS

I REACH OUT TO HOLD YOU,
BUT YOU AREN'T HERE.
I LOOK FOR YOU,
BUT, I CAN'T FIND YOU ANYWHERE!
I MUST HAVE DREAMED
THAT YOU WERE HERE
BECAUSE I FELT
A LITTLE TEAR,
A GENTLE TEAR
UPON MY FACE.
RUNNING DOWN,
IN SAD DISGRACE.
BECAUSE YOU ARE NOT HERE.
I CAN'T FIND YOU ANYWHERE!
TO HOLD ME.
TO LOVE ME.
BUT YOU'RE NOT HERE!
I'VE LOOKED FOR YOU-----BUT-
I CAN'T FIND YOU ANYWHERE!

August 1975/kesha laine.

TWILIGHT HOURS

IN THE LONG, DARK, AND LONELY HOURS,
I HAVE SAT AND WAITED FOR YOU
THE CLOCK LOUDLY TICKING AWAY
THE MINUTES, WITH NOTHING TO DO.
I SIT AND WATCH THE SHADOWS
OF THE NIGHT PASSING INTO DAY.
BUT I NEVER SEE THE SUNRISE-
BECAUSE THE CLOUDS WON'T GO AWAY.
IN THE EARLY AND DAMP HOURS
WHEN THE MOON HAS COMPLETELY GONE,
I STAND ALONE BY THE WINDOW
WAITING FOR THE DAWN.

1975 kesha

SLOWLY AND GENTLY

PLEASE GO AWAY
I KNOW I WOULD WANT YOU
FOR MORE THAN A DAY
SLOWLY AND GENTLY
PLEASE GO ON
I DON'T WANT YOU TO SEE
A CRYING WOMAN
SLOWLY AND GELTLY
PLEASE BE ON YOUR WAY.
I KNOW YOU REALLY
DON'T WANT TO STAY.
SLOWLY AND GENTLY
PLEASE SAY GOODNIGHT.
I DON'T WANT YOU HERE
WHEN I SEE THE SUNLIGHT.
SLOWLY AND GENTLY
PLEASE WALK AWAY
I CAN'T BEAR TO LOOK
AT THE BED WHERE WE LAY.

SLOWLY AND GENTLY
PLEASE WALK OUT OF MY LIFE.
I KNOW YOU DON'T WANT
ME FOR YOUR WIFE!
SLOWLY AND GENTLY
TELL ME GOODBYE
SLOWLY AND GENTLY,
SO I WON:T CRY>>>>>

KESHA

"ESCAPE"

I WANT TO GO HOME
I WANT TO WALK BAREFOOT IN THE GRASS.
AND WADE IN THE CREEK.
I WANT TO RUN THROUGH THE HILLS,
AND CLIMB IN THE TREES.
I WANT TO LOOK UP AND SEE CLEAR BLUE SKIES.
I WANT TO LISTEN TO THE BIRDS SING.
I WANT TO RUN WITH THE WIND.
AND WALK IN THE RAIN.
I WANT TO HEAR THE FROGS CROAK
AND LISTEN TO THE KADIDIES.
I WANT TO CATCH FIREFLIES
AND RACE JUNE BUGS.
I WANT TO SCROUNGE IN THE ATTIC.
AND LOOK AT OLD PICTURES.
I WANT TO SEE ALL MY OLD FRIENDS.
AND REMEMBER THE GOOD TIMES.
I WANT TO HOLD YOU IN MY ARMS.
AND TRY TO SHARE MY LIFE
I WANT TO FORGET THE HEARTACHE
AND LEARN TO LAUGH AGAIN.

I WANT TO GO HOME.

I WANT TO TRY TO RECAPTURE SOMETHING -

WHATEVER IT WAS THAT PASSED ME BY.

I WANT TO BE WHOLE AND ALIVE.

I WANT TO REACH OUT AND GRASP

THAT SOMETHING MISSING FROM MY SOUL.

IF ONLY I COULD GO BACK

BUT I CAN'T

I'VE ONLY GOT MY MEMORIES

AND A PAST I CAN'T CHANGE

ONLY A FUTURE, WHERE I CAN HOPE FOR

A LIFE WITHOUT PAIN.

MAY1976//KESHA LAINE.

NIGHT SHADOWS

THE MOON CASTS ITS SHADOW ACROSS THE FIELD.
IT IS BARREN FROM THE HARVEST
THERE IS DEW ON THE REMAINING CLOVER
AND IT SHINES IN THE MOONLIGHT LIKE TEARS.
I TRY TO IMAGINE MY TEARS AS THE DEW
AND THE DEW ON MY FACE.
AS I FEEL BARREN AND EMPTY
LIKE THIS DESERTED FIELD.
IT IS QUIET NOW. TOO QUIET.
AND THE SILENCE IS UNSETTLING ON MY MIND.
I AM TROUBLED BY MANY PAINFUL THOUGHTS
AND MY SCREAMS OF PAIN ECHO IN THE SILENT NIGHT.
SHATTERING THE PEACEFUL QUIET OF THE NIGHT.
BOUNCING OFF THE NAKED TREES
AND DROWNING IN THE COLD, RUSHING STREAMS.
AS I WALK INTO THE WATER
I AM SHOCKED BY THE PAINFUL COLDNESS
THAT SEEMS SO REFRESHING AT THE SAME TIME.
I FEEL THE SHARP ROCKS CUTTING MY FEET
AND THE WARM TRICKLE OF BLOOD MINGLE
AND POLLUTE THE WATER.
I SEE THE RED OF IT FROM THE MOON'S REFLECTION
AND I KNOW, IT IS THE BLEEDING OF MY HEART
ACHING FROM THE ABSENCE OF YOU.

July 13, 1975/kesha

SUMMER NIGHTS

THESE SUMMER NIGHTS
I'M ALL ALONE.
I THINK OF YOU
AND START TO PHONE.
BUT CHANGE MY MIND.
I REMEMBER YESTERDAY
WHEN YOU WERE HERE
BUT COULDN'T STAY
YOU HAD TO GO
SO FAR AWAY.
I HAD TO WAIT
FOR DAYS AND DAYS.
THESE SUMMER NIGHTS
I NEED YOU NOW.
BUT YOU ARE GONE.
AND I AM SO DOWN
I WANT YOU SO,
AND I Can't WAIT
UNTIL YOU ARE MINE.
ALL MY OWN
THESE SUMMER NIGHTS.

Aug
kesha

BROWN EYES

I THOUGHT I HAD MET YOU
SOMEWHERE BEFORE.
WALKING DOWN THE STREET
OR PASSING THROUGH A DOOR.
I THOUGHT YOU HAD HELD ME
A FEW NIGHTS BEFORE,
BUT, I QUESS I AM MISTAKEN.
I DIDN'T KNOW THERE WERE MORE.
BROWN EYES
WHO COME AROUND TO LOVE YOU
WHEN YOU AREN'T PREPARED
TO GIVE IN TO SOMEONE
WHO REALLY DOESN'T CARE.
I THOUGHT I HAD LOVED YOU
SOMETIMES BEFORE,
BUT NOW THAT I SEE YOU MORE CLEARLY,
I KNOW I WOULD HAVE WANTED MORE.

NOVEMBER 1975
KESHA LAINE./KAREN HOLSINGER.

HOPE

I KEEP LOOKING UP
HOPING TO SEE YOU WALK BY
I FINALLY SEE YOU, YOU SMILE
AND I SIGH.
I TURN AROUND TO FOLLOW YOU
AS YOU WALK ON DOWN THE FLOOR
SOMETIMES YOU LOOK BACK AT ME
BUT I REALLY DON'T KNOW WHAT FOR.
I KEEP HOPING YOU'LL TALK TO ME
TELL ME WHAT I WANT TO HEAR
BUT HOW CAN YOU, WHEN
IM AFRAID TO TELL YOU HOW I FEEL.
MY FACE GROWS HOT AS I FEEL YOU LOOK AT ME
MY HEART GOES WILD, THE CLOSER YOU COME TO ME.
I WISH I COULD REACH OUT AND TOUCH YOU
OR TELL YOU HOW I FEEL.

MAYBE IF I SMILE ONE MORE TIME
YOU'LL TELL ME WHAT I NEED TO HEAR.

DECEMBER 17.1975

IMAGE

I THINK OF YOU AND TRY TO MAKE OUT YOUR FACE
THAT HAS BECOME SO HAZY IN MY MIND
I TRY TO REMEMBER HOW HAPPY WE WERE THEN
YOU WERE SO WARM, GENTLE AND KIND.

I TRY TO IMAGINE HOW I WOULD REACT
IF I FINALLY SAW YOU AGAIN.
IF I WOULD CRY OR LAUGH.
OR JUST STARE IN DISBELIEF.

I WONDER WHAT IT WOULD BE LIKE
TO HAVE YOU TOUCH ME NOW
IT'S BEEN SO LONG
I WONDER IF I WOULD KNOW YOU AT ALL.

JANUARY 1976
KESHA LAINE.

LAST CHAPTER

IN THE DARK AND STORMY PAGES OF MY MIND
I TURN BACK AND REMEMBER THE
MEN I THOUGHT I'D LOVED.
BUT NOW, I KNOW YOU:
AND I WISH I'D NEVER KNOWN ANYONE ELSE BEFORE.

BUT HOW COULD I BEGIN TO IMAGINE I'D EVER
FINE SOMEONE LIKE YOU.
HOW WAS I TO KNOW?
THAT YOU'D REALLY CARE FOR ME TOO?

IN THE WORN AND TORN PAGES
IN THE BOOK OF FORGIVEN SINS,
I CLOSE THE COVER TO END THIS CHAPTER
AND WISH I COULD START OVER AGAIN.

FEB.1976
KESHA LAINE.

ANXIETY

I SIT IN THE QUIET DARKNESS
AND I THINK OF YOU.
AND I WANT SO MUCH TO REACH OUT
AND TOUCH YOU.

I NEED TO HOLD YOU
AND TELL YOU HOW I FEEL
BUT I ALWAYS GET SO SCARED
WHENEVER YOU GET NEAR.

I'M AFRAID YOU MIGHT SEE
JUST HOW MUCH I NEED YOU
AND YOU WOULD GO AWAY.
FRIGHTENED BY THE LOVE I COULD GIVE YOU.

FEB.1976
KESHA LAINE.

CONSUMED

HONEY, I LOVE YOU.
I THINK ABOUT YOU ALL THE TIME.
I DREAM ABOUT YOU EVERY NIGHT,
YOU ARE CONSTANTLY ON MY MIND.
I WAS ALONE AND SCARED WHEN I MET YOU.
AND I NEEDED YOUR LOVE SO MUCH.
NOW, EVERY TIME I SEE YOU
MY BODY ACHES FOR YOUR TOUCH.
UNTIL THE DAY I MET YOU,
I ALWAYS FELT SO SAD.
BUT NOW THAT I KNOW AND LOVE YOU.
MY LIFE DOESN'T SEEM SO BAD.
MY NEED FOR YOU KEEPS GROWING,
LIKE THE LOVE THAT'S IN MY HEART.
AND EVERY DAY I WANT YOU MORE.
PLEASE, LET ME TOUCH YOUR HEART.
REACH OUT AND TAKE ME, DARLING
LOVE ME ONE MORE TIME
LET ME TOUCH YOUR HEART AND SOUL.
PLEASE, LET ME MAKE YOU MINE.

FEB. 1975/KESHA LAINE.

INSOMNIA

IN THE LONLINESS OF THE NIGHT
THE NIGHTS WITHOUT YOU
I LAY AWAKE IN BED
CAN'T GET TO SLEEP WITHOUT YOU.
I MISS YOUR ARMS AROUND ME
HOLDING ME SO TIGHT.
I NEED TO SEE YOU THERE BESIDE ME,
COME THE MORNING LIGHT.
I NEED TO HAVE YOU NEAR ME
CAN'T STAND IT WHEN YOU ARE AWAY
I HOPE YOU COME BACK TOMORROW
CAN'T TAKE IT ANOTHR DAY!
COME LAY BESIDE ME
GENTLY TOUCH MY FACE
TAKE ME IN YOUR ARMS
SHOW ME LOVES GENTLE WAYS.
TENDERLY LIE BESIDE ME
PUT MY MIND AT EASE
STAY UNTIL I'M FAST ASLEEP
DON'T LEAVE UNTIL MORNING, PLEASE.

APRIL 1976/KESHA LAINE.E

SOUL LESS

AS THE NIGHT BECOMES DARK
THE FEARS BEGIN TO QUELL UP IN MY
HEART AND SOUL
MY MIND BECOMES FILLED WITH DOUBTS
ABOUT MY LOVING YOU.

JUST AS MY VISION BECOMES HINDERED IN THE NIGHT
MY MEMORY HAS BECOME FADED AND DULL
I BECOME FRIGHTENED BY THE THINGS I CANNOT SEE.

I FEEL AN OVER POWERING SENSE ABOUT ME
LIKE A SHADOW SOMEWHERE-
MY SOUL-WAITING, WANTING
TO BECOME ONE WITH ME.
WHILE I AM WAITING, WANTING TO
BECOME ONE WITH YOU.

FEB.1975/KESHA LAINE

SENSELESS

SLEEPLESS NIGHTS AND RESTLESS DAYS
ARE ALL I'VE HAD SINCE YOU WENT AWAY.
LONELY STREETS AND VACANT LOTS
ARE ALL I SEE, BUT YOU ARE ALWAYS IN MY THOUGHTS.

I THINK OF YOU BOTH DAY AND NIGHT,
AND I OFTEN WONDER IF WHAT I DID WAS RIGHT.

I SIT AROUND AND MOPE AND MOAN,
CRYING MY EYES OUT BECAUSE
I'M ALL ALONE:

BUT I KNOW THAT THIS WAY IS
BETTER THAN THE OTHER.
BECAUSE, YOU SEE, I HAD TAKEN ANOTHER LOVER.

FEB.1976
KESHA LKAINE.

LONG OVER

IT'S BEEN SO LONG SINCE I HAVE TOUCHED YOU.
WE'VE BEEN APART SO LONG.
I WONDER IF YOU'VE CHANGED MUCH,
AND IF OUR LOVE WAS WRONG.

WE HAD SO MANY HOPES AND DREAMS.
WE CRAMMED A LIFETIME INTO DAYS.
YOU SWORE YOU'D NEVER LOVED THIS WAY BEFORE,
AND I WAS AFRAID TO LOVE YOU, BECAUSE I KNEW
YOU WERE GOING AWAY.

WE'VE KEPT IN TOUCH, THROUGH MILES APART,
AND PLANNED OUR FUTURE TOGETHER.
NOW THAT OUR TIME HAS COME,
I WONDER IF YOU CAN LOVE ME FOREVER.

FEB.76
KESHA LAINE.

ONCE, AGAIN

HERE I AM AGAIN, DARLING.
LYING ALL ALONE.
WONDERING WHERE YOU ARE.
AND IF YOU ARE ALONE.
IT SEEMS I'M ALWAYS WAITING
FOR YOU TO COME SEE ME
I'M WAITING FOR THE LONGEST TIME
AND I WONDER WHERE YOU COULD BE
I KNOW YOU ARE A BUSY MAN
TRYING TO MAKE A GOOD LIFE.
BUT I DON'T THINK YOU WILL EVER
FIND THE TIME TO MAKE ME YOUR WIFE.
YOU TELL ME TO HAVE PATIENCE
THINGS WILL WORK OUT SOON
BUT YOU DON'T SEEM TO UNDERSTAND
IT'S BEEN A YEAR YOU'VE BEEN PLAYIING THIS TUNE
YOU KEEP SAYING THAT I WANT A LOT
BUT, ALL I WANT IS YOU.

I'VE TRIED EVERYTHING I CAN THINK OF
I DON'T KNOW WHAT ELSE TO DO
EVERY DAY AND NIGHT
I SIT HERE AND WAIT FOR YOU.
CAN'T YOU SEE OR UNDERSTAND
ALL THE LOVE I HAVE FOR YOU
I JUST WANT YOUR LAUGHTER
YOUR SMILES AND TEARS.
I WANT YOUR HOPES AND DREAMS……..
I EVEN WANT YOUR FEARS
I WANT YOU TO WANT ME
AS MUCH AS I WANT YOU.
AND, I NEED FOR YOU TO LOVE ME
AT LEAST HALF AS MUCH AS I LOVE YOU.

OCTOBER 10, 1976
KESHA LAINE.

COLD AND BARE

WINTER IS COMING
SO COLD AND SO GRAY
JUST LIKE MY HEART
SINCE YOUR LOVE WENT AWAY.
I NEED SOMETHING STRONG
BUT THE WIND WON"T DO
I NEED ARMS AROUND ME
THAT BELONG TO YOU.
I WANT TO SEE THE SUN
NOT THE CLOUDS AND SNOW.
I WANT TO GO ON LIVING
BUT I NEED TO KNOW.
IS THERE SOMETHING
OR SOMEONE OUT THERE
WITH WHOM I CAN SHARE
OR MUST I GO ON LIVING A LIFE THAT IS BARE.?

NOV. 1976/KESHA LAINE

SILENT NIGHT

IN THE SILENCE OF THE DARKNESS,
I LAY ALONE.
I REACH OUT INTO THE NIGHT
BUT YOU AREN'T THERE!
IN THE STILLNESS OF THE NIGHT
I WANT TO HOLD YOU.
BUT I DON'T EVEN KNOW
WHERE YOU HAVE GONE.
I LOOK UP INTO THE SKY
BUT, THERE IS NO MOON OR STARS.
EVERYTHING AROUND ME
IS DEAD AND COLD!
THERE IS NO WIND, NO RAY OF LIGHT,
THERE IS NO LIVING!
I HEAR NO TALKING,
NOT EVEN A WHISPER
THERE IS NO BREATHING
JUST THE DEATHLY SILENCE OF MY LOVES.
AND THEN, THE HAUNTING LAUGHTER OF MY PAST!
SOMEONE, PLEASE HELP ME!

PLEASE WAKE ME FROM THIS DREAM!
I AM CRYING AND I AM SO SORRY!
GOD! PLEASE FORGIVE ME FOR WHAT I'VE DONE
IN THE SILENCE OF THE NIGHT
I CALL OUT YOUR NAME.
And in the stillness of the night........................
I KILL THE PAIN!

Oct. 1974/kesha

BELIVE

I BELIEVE IN SUNSHINE
AND I BELIEVE IN RAIN.
I BELIEVE THERE IS A REASON
FOR EVERY LIVING THING.
I BELIEVE IN COURAGE.
AND I BELIEVE IN CHANGE.
I BELIEVE IN THE FAMILIAR
EVERYTHING IS NEW, NOT STRANGE
I BELIEVE IN FREEDOM
AND I BELIEVE IN HOPE
I BELIEVE WE'RE GONA MAKE IT!
ALL WE HAVE TO DO, IS COPE.
I BELIEVE IN TODAY.
AND I BELIEVE INTOMORROW.
I BELIEVE OUR HAPPINESS]
WILL OVERRULE OUR SORROW.
I BELIEVE IN PASSION
AND I BELIEVE IN LOVE.
I BELIEVE IN HEAVEN
AND A GOD ABOVE.
I BELIEVE THERE IS A REASON
FOR EVERYTHING WE DO
BUT MOST OF ALL, MY DARLING:
I BELIEVE IN YOU.

Sept 1974 KESHA

MY THOUGHTS ON LONLINESS

YESTERDAY I WAS ALONE.
IN SILENT AND VIOLENT PAIN.
TODAY I AM ALONE.
BUT BELIEVE I'M A BIT MORE SANE.
TOMORROW, I WILL BE ALONE.
SO TELL ME, WHAT DID I GAIN?

.............Kesha Laine

OVER

I CLOSE MY EYES,
BUT MY MEMORY OF YOU IS FAINT
YOUR BLUE EYES AREN'T SO SHINY
AND YOUR SMILE IS
NOT SO BRIGHT.
COULD IT BE THAT I AM FINALLY
GETTING OVER YOU?
OR HAS IT BEEN THAT LONG?
WHATEVER THE REASON, I DON'T CARE!
JUST AS LONG AS YOU DON'T COME BACK!!

kes

Who?

I'VE GROWN TOO OLD FOR THIS
GAME OF ONE NIGHT STANDS.
AND I AM LOOKING FOR A SPECIAL KIND OF MAN.
I'M NOT ASKING FOR A LOT, JUST ONE OF MY OWN.
BECAUSE I AM SO TIRED OF BEING ALONE.

Kesha Laine

Not him

SWEAR ME NO OATHES, MY LOVE.
SPARE ME FROM THE PAIN OF DECEIT
MAKE ME NO RAINBOW BELIEVER, MY LOVE.
DON'T FILL MY HEART WITH HOPE.
DON'T TELL ME THINGS YOU DON'T MEAN
AND I WILL PRETEND
THAT YOU ARE MINE TO KEEP.

KESHA

Misery

BLACK AS THE NIGHT YOUR SOUL IS.
STORMY GRAY ARE YOUR EYES.
COLD AS A STONE YOUR HEART IS
SO BE IT TIL THE DAY YOU DIE.

LONELY RAMBLINGS

TAKE AWAY M Y LONLINESS AND PAIN
FULFILL MY SOUL AND LET ME LIVE AGAIN
TAKE ME IN YOUR ARMS AND KISS MY LIPS
FREE MY MIND AND SHOW ME WHAT I'VE MISSED.
TAKE ME AS YOUR LOVER AND MEND MY HEART
LOVE THIS LONELY WOMAN, AND GIVE ME A BRAND
NEW START.
IT IS SO QUIET. SO VERY PEACEFUL. I CAN HEAR THE
BEATING OF MY HEART.
HOW VERY STRANGE, HOW ODD,
THIS CONSTRASTING TO THE PAIN
THAT IS TEARING ME APART.

Kesha Laine

Forgiveness

LOVE, PLEASE COME TO ME.
I AM SO LONELY
LOVE, COME SURROUND ME.
COME HOLD ME TIGHT.
LOVE, PLEASE COME TO ME.
COME TO ME TONIGHT.

1973/KESHA LAINE.

***

LAMENTING SONG

GIVE ME SOME WARM, TENDER LOVING AND I WILL BE FINE.
GIVE ME SOME WARM, TENDER LOVING ALL NIGHT LONG.
WITH A MAN LIKE YOU, TO HELP ME THROUGH THESE
LONELY NIGHTS
GIVE ME SOMEWARM, TENDER LOVING AND I'LL BE FINE.

I'LL GIVE YOU SOME WARM, TENDER LOVING IF YOU WILL
BE MINE.
I'll GIVE YOU SOME WARM, TENDER LOVING ALL THE TIME.
WITH A MAN LIKE YOU, TO SEE ME THROUGH THESE
TRYING TIMES.
I'll GIVE YOU SOME WARM, TENDER LOVING IF YOU WILL
BE MINE.

kes

SEPARATE VACATIONS

I THOUGHT YOU DIDN'T MATTER SO MUCH TO M E.
WHEN YOU WENT AWAY AND WAS GONE FOR A WHILE-
I FELT OK, I THOUGHT I WAS FREE.
BUT YOU CAME BACK.
ONE LOOK IS ALL IT TOOK
MY EYES FILLED WITH TEARS
LIKE A ROLLING BROOK.
I WANTED TO REACH OUT AND TOUCH YOU AGAIN.
BUT I WAS AFRAID I'D FEEL THAT LOVE FOR YOU AGAIN.
EACH TIME I SEE YOU, MY POOR HEART IS TORN.
AND WHEN I SEE YOU WITH HER,
I WISH I'D NEVER BEEN BORN.

kesha

MEMBERENCES

I REMEMBER LAYING IN YOUR ARMS
AND LOVING YOU ALL NIGHT LONG.
GENTLY CARRESSING YOU,-
AND SILENTLY RESTING IN EACH OTHERS ARMS.
I REMEMBER HOW GOOD IT FELT
TO HAVE YOU LOVE ME BACK.
HOLDING ME SO TENDERLY,
THEN DRIFTING OFF TO SLEEP.
I RMEMBER HOW MUCH I MISSED YOU
EVEN THOUGH YOU WEREN'T GONE LONG.
BUT I MISS YOU MORE NOW-
BECAUSE WHILE YOU ARE HERE WITH ME,
YOUR HEART AND MIND ARE LOVING SOMEONE ELSE.

AUGUS 1975 DF
KESHA LAINE

Young Lad

I ADMIRE YOU FROM A DISTANCE.
YOUR BODY LOOKS SO FINE.
I WISH I COULD GET CLOSER
BUT I WILL HAVE TO BIDE MY TIME.

IT WONT BE LONG BEFORE YOU LEAVE.
I WISH YOU DIDN'T HAVE TO GO.
BUT YOU ARE SO YOUNG,
AND YOU HAVE MANY THINGS TO DO.

YOUR BLUE, BLUE EYES JUST MAKE ME MELT.
YOUR SMILE PUTS SUNSHINE IN MY SOUL.
I WANT YOU SO VERY MUCH.
I WISH YOU DIDN'T HAVE TO GO.

I LOVE IT WHEN YOU LAUGH
IT FEELS MY HEART WITH JOY.
I WISH THAT I COULD HOLD YOU
BUT YOU ARENT YET A MAN.
YOU ARE MERELY A SWEET, INNOCENT BOY.

Kesha/august 1977

LIFE SOURCE

WHEN I LOOK AT YOU, I FEEL SO ALIVE AND WARM.
I FEEL LIKE A REAL WOMAN.

MY PULSE RACES, MY BREATH GETS LIGHT
I CAN SEE NO ONE BUT YOU.

MY MIND THINKS ONLY OF YOU.
MY HEART KNOWS ONLY YOUR LOVE.
MY DESIRE FOR YOU IS SO STRONG.

I COLLASPE IN YOUR EMBRACE
YOU SURROUND MY ENTIRE BEING.
YOU ARE MY LIFE
PLEASE DON'T TAKE IT AWAY.

AUGUST 1977/KESHA LAINE.

WISHFUL WOUGHT

ALL MY LIFE I HAVE WALKED ALONG TINY
PATHS COVERED WITH STONES.
I HAVE LIVED A QUIET LIFE. ALWAYS
PREPARING TO BECOME A WIFE.
I NEVER ASKED FOR MUCH, AND OFTEN GOTTEN LESS
I TRIED TO BE GOOD, BUT MY LIFE IS SUCH A MESS.
I TRY SO HARD TO ALWAYS PLEASE -
TO MAKE THEM HAPPY.
BUT THEY ALWAYS SEEM TO LEAVE.
I AM SO TIRED OF FIGHTING, AND I
WANT TO LIE DOWN AND DIE.
BUT THERE HAS TO BE SOMEONE OUT
THERE, WHO WONT SAY GOOD BYE.
SO, I WILL TRY ONE MORE DAY. JUST
TO SEE IF IT IS ANY BETTER.
IF IT ISN'T, GOD, THEN YOU CAN JUST FORGET IT.!

AUGUST 26,77/KESHA LAINE.

TORTURE

WHY DO YOU TORTURE ME?
AFTER ALL THESE YEARS?
WHY COME BACK INTO MY LIFE,
STIRRING UP MIXED EMOTIONS AND FEAR.
YOUR MEMORY HAS BARELY HAUNTED ME

ACROSS THE MANY MILES.
NOW THAT I HAVE ALMOST FORGOTTEN YOU,
YOU SHOW UP WITH THAT SILLY SMILE.
WHAT DO YOU WANT FROM ME?

I HAVE NOTHING LEFT TO GIVE.
MEN LIKE YOU HAVE STRIPPED MY SOUL
MAKING ME NOT WANT TO LIVE.
MY LIFE HAS BEEN SO ROCKY,
FILLED WITH HEART ACHES AND PAIN.
WHY DID YOU COME BACK FOR?
WHAT DID YOU EXPECT TO GAIN?

GO ON!! GET OUT OF MY LIFE!!
PUT DOWN MY HEART.
PLEASE PUT A PAINLESS END
TO SOMETHING WE SHOULD'T EVEN START...

kesha

LONG DISTANCE LOVER

HOW COME YOU ARE NOT HERE TO HOLD ME?
WHEN I NEED YOU SO MUCH?
WHEN I FEEL THE WORLD'S WEIGHT
UPON MY SHOULDERS.
HOW COME YOU ARENT" HERE TO HELP?
HELP PICK UP THE ROCKS THAT LAY IN MY PATH.
AND MAKE SURE THERE ARE ONLY
GOOD THINGS AHEAD.
TO HELP SOOTHE OUT THE BAD THINGS
AND TO KEEP ME FROM HARM
AND WHERE THERE IS DARKNESS, SHOW ME A LIGHT.
SO I WON'T BE AFRAID IN MY LIFE.
HOW COME YOU AREN'T HERE?
WHEN I FEEL SO HELPLESS, AND ALONE.
WHEN I FEEL SO LOST AND DESERTED?
WHERE ARE YOU, WHEN I NEED YOU? LIKE NOW.?

MAY 1977/KESHA LAINE

EMPTY HOUSE

OH, THESE DARKENED HOLLOW HALLS.
THESES EMPTY ROOMS WITHIN MY HOUSE.
THE SILENCE IS SO DEAFENING.
OH GOD! WHERE IS THE LAUGHTER?
I READ MY MAGAZINES, THEN WATCH T. V.
I DON'T FEEL LIKE EATING.
IT IS SUCH A WASTE; JUST FOR ME. DON'T YOU SEE?
I LISTEN TO MUSIC,
BUT THE WORDS DON'T RHYME.
SO I TURN UP THE VOLUME
TO DROWN OUT MY CRYING.
I PULL DOWN THE SHADES
AND SIT IN THE DARK
I TRY TO FORGET
THE PAIN IN MY HEART.
MY SOUL IS SO EMPTY.
I AM JUST A HOLLOW SHELL.
I NEED SOMEONE TO COME
COMFORT ME
AND FREE ME FROM THIS
LIVING HELL!

Kesha

FAREWELL

GOODBYE, SWEET LOVE.
I REALLY DON'T WANT TO GO.
OUR LOVE HAS BEEN SO GOOD
BUT IT ISNT ENOUGH, YOU KNOW.

SO LONG, SWEET DREAMS
I HAD OF YOUR COMING HOME.
TO HOLD ME IN YOUR ARMS
BUT YOU'D RATHER
HAVE THE WORLD TO ROAM.

GOOD NIGHT, SWEET MEMORIES.
I'LL TRY TO CLOSE THE DOOR.
BECAUSE NO MATTER HOW HARD WE TRIED
IT WOULD NEVER BE LIKE BEFORE.

UNTIL TOMORROW, SWEET DARLING.
THAT'S WHAT I'D LIKE TO SAY.
I KNOW DEEP WITHIN MY HEART
THIS IS THE ONLY WAY.

GOODBYE, SWEET LOVE,
GRIEVE NOT LONG FOR ME.
YOU'LL FIND ANOTHER, MY LOVE.
SOME ONE MUCH BETTER THAN ME.!

April76
kesha

END OF DAY

THE SUN SETTING BEHIND THE
HILLS, SLOWLY SINKING.
THE LAST RAYS FADING WITH THE CLOUDS.
IT REMINDS ME OF MYSELF.
MY LIFE SLOWLY DESOLVING AND
WASTING INTO NOTHING.
BECAUSE I'VE THROWN IT ALL AWAY.
BY TRYING TOO HARD TO PLEASE
I DROVE YOU AWAY.
THEN WHEN YOU WANTED TO COME BACK,
I MET YOU WITH ANOTHER MAN.
YOU MISUNDERSTOOD MY WEAKNESS
FOR INDEPENDENCE,
AND LEFT ME ALONE AGAIN.
I'M SORRY IF YOU THINK I'VE BETRAYED YOU.
PLEASE, DON'T THINK BAD OF ME:
BECAUSE I LOVED HIM TOO.
IT WAS JUST BECAUSE I NEEDED LOVE,
AND YOU HAD BEEN GONE SO LONG.

PLEASE, TRY TO REALIZE THE PAIN
I HAVE BEEN GOING THROUGH,
BEING AFRAID THAT I MIGHT LOOSE YOU
JUST BECAUSE I LET HIM TOUCH MY HEART,
DOESN'T MEAN HE OWNS MY SOUL.
PLEASE TRY TO UNDERSTAND THAT WHILE
YOU THOUGHT I WAS BEING UNTRUE:
I WAS ONLY DOING WHAT YOU WERE DOING TOO!

FEB.77/KESHA

SCRAPBOOK

THE BOOK IS OLD AND RAGGED.
ITs PAGES TORN AND YELLOWED.
STAINED AND CRACKED BY MANY YEARS
LIKE A GOOD WINE, IT'S MELLOWED
IT HOLDS PICTURES OF SPECIAL DAYS
AND PAPERS THAT WERE THOUGHT IMPORTANT.
A FOUR LEAF CLOVER, A ROSE PETAL, AND AN
OLD GET WELL CARD
FROM SOMEONE LONG FORGOTTEN.
A FEW PICTURES HAVE COME UNGLUED,
THEIR NAMES ARE BLURRED OR WORN AWAY.
A FEW I KNOW I NEVER KNEW,
BUT THIS ONE I SAW JUST YESTERDAY.
I TURN THE PAGES ONE BY ONE.
AND TOWARD THE BACK I FIND
ONE OF YOU.
AND SUDDENDLY MEMORIES
COME FLOODING TO MY MIND.
I SIT AND LOOK, AND TRY TO FEEL
THE WAY I FELT BACK THEN.
BUT SOMEHOW I KNOW THAT I'LL
NEVER BE ABLE TO LOVE LIKE THAT AGAIN.

02/04/1976/KESHA LAINE.

TRAFFIC

CARS GOING DOWN THE STREET
THEIR HONKING HORNS BLASTING INTO
MY PAINFUL THOUGHTLESS MIND.
SPEEDING PAST ME, SHARPLY TURNING CORNERS
NEVER GIVING A SIGNAL TO CAUTION ME.

CARS GOING DOWN THE STREET
THEIR TIRES SMACKING THE PAVEMENT.
MAKING WHISTLING SOUNDS
AS THEY GO THROUGH THE
HOLLOW DARKEN TUNNELS OF MY SOUL.

CARS GOING DOWN THE STREET
GOING EVERYWHERE AND NOWHERE
IN PARTICULAR,
JUST GETTING OUT AND GOING PAST ME.
NEVER THINKING TO STOP AND ASK
IF I WOULD LIKE TO GO TOO.

CARS GOING DOWN THE STREET.
MUSIC SEEPING FROM THE WINDOWS.
LEAVING JUST A HINT OF LIFE
SOMEWHERE ELSE, WITH SOMEONE ELSE.
THEN GOING ON
WITHOUT ME.

JAN. 4,1976kesha

THE TOUCHING OF YOU.

I LAY AT NIGHT AND DREAM OF YOU
I SEE YOUR FACE, THOUGH HAZY,
ACROSS THE MANY MILES.
I AM STIRRED FROM MY SOFT SLUMBER
AND I KNOW:
IT IS JUST THE TOUCHING OF YOU.
I WALK ALONE THROUGH THE MEADOWS.
AND A SOFT, WARM BREEZE SURROUNDS ME.
THE SUN SHINES WARM UPON MY FACE.
AND I KNOW:
IT IS JUST THE TOUCHING OF YOU.
I LOOK OUT INTO THE DARK NIGHT SKIES.
AND TRY TO COUNT THE STARS.
I HEAR A WHISPER, EVER SO FAINT
BRUSH PAST MY EAR.
AND I KNOW:
IT IS JUST THE TOUCHING OF YOU.
I SIT OUTSIDE AND LISTEN TO THE CROAKING FROGS
THEN COMES THE RAIN. THE GENTLE, WARM RAIN.

MINGLING WITH MY TEARS, FALLING UPON MY CHEEK.
AND I KNOW:
IT IS JUST THE TOUCHING OF YOU.
I THINK BACK AND REMEMBER
ALL THE TIMES BEFORE.
LIKE SNAPSHOTS WORN AND FADED.
OLD LOVE LETTERES, WITH PAGES TORN
NOW I KNOW WHY THEY NEVER MATTERED…
IT WASN'T THE TOUCHING OF YOU.

kesha

ABSENTEE LOVER

WHERE ARE YOU, MY DARLING.
WHEN I NEED YOU TO HOLD ME TIGHT?
ARE YOU WITH SOMEONE ELSE
WHILE I'M HERE ALONE TONIGHT.?

WHERE ARE YOU, MY DARLING
WHEN I NEED TO HEAR SOFT WORDS?
ARE YOU REALLY WORKING,
WOULD YOU BE HERE IF YOU COULD?

WHERE ARE YOU, MY DARLING
WHEN THE SUN WAKES ME UP ALONE?
IF YOU REALLY COULD"T MAKE IT,
WHY DIDN'T YOU THINK TO PHONE?

WHERE ARE YOU, MY DARLING
WHILE I SIT HERE AND QUIETLY WAIT?
ARE YOU COMING HOME AT ALL?
OR IS IT ALREADY TOO LATE?

KES

THEIF, REVISITED

I FEEL YOU EYES GLIDE OVER MY BODY.,
FALLING DOWN
AND SOFTLY CARRESSING MY BREASTS
I SEE THE WANT RISE IN YOUR BLOODSHOT EYES.
AND I UNDERSTAND YOUR NEED FOR ME.
I KNOW THE URGENT DESIRE THAT IS
FLARING UP IN YOUR SOUL.
I FEEL THE FIRE FROM YOUR HEART IGNITE
AND IT BURNS A HOLE IN ME.

I FEEL THE VIBRATIONS
AS I SEE THE LUST RISE UP
AND TAKE CONTROL OF YOUR SOUL.
I SEE THE VISIONS THAT MUST
DANCE THROUGHOUT YOUR MIND.
YOUR EYES STOP TO GLARE AT MY DRESS
SOFTLY CLINGING TO MY THIGHS
I FEEL THE PRESSURE OF YOUR ARMS AROUND ME
AS YOU PUSH ME DOWN UPON THE FLOOR.
YOU ROB ME OF MY VIRTURES
MAKING ME A COMMON WHORE.

May 1997/kesha

SHATTERED DREAMS

I ONCE HELD DREAMS SO FOND AND CLEAR
I DREAMED OF A BABY GIRL SO NEAR
WITH TWINKLING EYES AND ROSEY CHEEKS
AND A SMILING FACE, WITH HAIR SO FAIR.

BUT MY DREAMS WERE BROKEN
SO DRASTIC AND UNFAIR!
REALITY IS SO HARSH,
TOO MUCH TO BEAR.

PIERCING LIGHTNING STRUCK DOWN
THROUGH MY SOUL
AND THUNDER CLOUDS RAN PAST MY EYES.
MY DREAMS ONCE BRIGHT, ARE SHATTERED AND GONE
WITH NO RAINBOW TO GAZE AT, AFTER THE STORM

I HAVE AN EMPTY AND ACHING SOUL,
WITH WARM ARMS THAT YEARN TO HOLD
A BABE ONCE MORE.
MY EYES ARE CLOUDED WITH TEARS SO COLD
THAT MATCH THE HOLE THAT IS IN MY SOUL.

kesha

I WROTE THIS AFTER ANOTHER MISCARRAGE//JULY 22, 1985. A YEAR LATER, JULY 16, 1986, I HAD A SON, Mark- AND I AM SO THANKFULL FOR HIM.

THROUGH A MOTHERS EYE

KISSING FRECKELS ON HIS FACE.
MISCHIEVIOUS EYES,
AND A HINT OF A SMILE.
I SEE YOU CRAWLING, WALKING
AND RUNNING THROUGH YOUR LIFE
SO BUSY
I HEAR YOUR LAUGHTER
I REMEMBER YOUR TEARS, AND
HOLDING YOU AND ROCKING YOU
FEVER'S BROKEN
YOU ARE FINALLY SLEEPING
EXHAUSTED AS I WAS
I COULDN'T PUT YOU DOWN
SUCH AN ANGELIC FACE, WITH
TINY FINGERS WRAPPED AROUND MINE
MAKING MY HEART SO FULL OF LOVE.
I SEE YOU GROWING OLDER
I SEE THE WHISPERS TO YOUR FRIENDS.

I SEE YOUR CROOKED SMILE
YOU GIVE YOUR CURRENT GIRLFRIEND.
THEN AGAIN, I REMEMBER
YOUR SWEET BABY FACE.
YOUR SKINNED KNEES
HUGS AND KISSES FOR YOUR MOMMA
FINDING ANOTHER HOLE IN YOUR JEANS.
MY LITTLE BOY HAS GROWN UP SO FAST
AND HE WILL BE GONE IN A FLASH…

KEHA (joe)

LOVE BANDIT

(A SONG I WROTE TO MY FIRST SON, WILLIAM JOESPH)
1979-1980*

RUNNING DOWN THE HALLWWAYS
CLIMBING ON THE CHAIRS.
PULLING THINGS OUT OF THE CABINET
THAT'S MY SWEETHEART.
THAT'S MY LITTLE BOY.
THAT'S MY LOVE BANDIT.
CLIMBING ON THE TABLE
LOOKING OUT THE WINDOW
WANTING TO GO OUT AND PLAY
THAT'S MY SWEETHEART
THAT'S MY LITTLE BOY.
THAT'S MY LOVE BANDIT
HERE A CAR
THERE A TRUCK
CRAYONS ALL OVER THE FLOOR
JUST WHEN I'M ABOUT TO YELL,
I SEE THAT TWINKLE IN HIS EYES
AND THAT CUTE LITTLE SMILE.

RUNNING DOWN THE HALLWAYS
CLIMBING ON THE CHAIRS
PULLING THINGS OUT OF THE CABINET
THAT'S MY SWEETHEART
THAT'S MY LITTLE BOY.
THAT'S MY LOVE BANDIT
STEALING ALL MY KISSES
STEALING ALL MY HUGS
STEALING MY HEART AWAY
BUT YOU THINK HE'S GOT
ME WRAPPED AROUND HIS LITTLE FINGER-
WELL, I WOULDN'T HAVE IT ANY OTHER WAY!
RUNNING DOWN THE HALLWAYS
CLIMBING ON THE CHAIRS
PULLING THINGS OUT OF THE CABINET
THAT'S MY SWEETHEART.
THAT'S MY LITTLE BOY
THAT'S MY LOVE BANDIT!

Written for my son, Willie Joe. //Kesha

MY WARD

I dream and think of you so often
From night into day and into night.
I glide from day to day
Hardly knowing or remembering
The trivial things I do.
But I would know your hint of a smile,
And the softness of your laughter,
And the eyes that used to care for me.
If I saw you in the midst of a thousand
I would know it
As I knew you then.
Before you went back to her.
Your wife.
After 18 months of my bliss
You are gone.
And my soul hurts so
Deeply.
I don't think I will ever
Get over losing you.

August 15/1997/kesha Laine

FRED TOO

When I dream of you
I feel sunshine warm all over
I imagine I'm lying in your arms
Cuddling and smiling up into
The warmth of your embrace.

Listening to your heartbeat.
As you move to kiss me
Your breath life into my mouth
Fulfilling my soul

Your hand so gently brushes against my face
Then you slowly caress my breast
My eyes flutter open
And I see your loving face.
And I know,
My dreams of you
Are true.

August 05,1997/kesha Laine.

PLEASE, BABY, PLEASE

MY ARMS ACHE TO HOLD YOU, HOLD YOU, HOLD YOU.
MY LIPS YEARN TO KISS YOUR SWEET MOUTH
MY HEART SKIPS A BEAT, AND MY MIND RUNS WILD
AS I REMEMBER THE WARMTH OF YOUR SMILE.
MY SENSES GO CRAZY, AS YOUR SCENT
LINGERS ON MY PILLOW.
AND I WONDER, IF YOU ARE LYING AWAKE
THINKING OF ME TONIGHT.
MY ARMS ACHE TO HOLD YOU, HOLD YOU, HOLD YOU.
I REMEMBER YOU DEEP HAZEL EYES.
MY BREATH HASTENS QUICKLY
AS I REMEMBER YOUR LOVING EMBRACE.
MY VISION OF YOU SLEEPING BESIDE ME
MAKES ME WONDER IF YOU EVER
LOVED LIKE THIS BEFORE.
IF ANY OTHER WOMAN WAS CURLED
UP IN YOUR ARMS.
MY ARMS ACHE TO HOLD YOU, HOLD YOU, HOLD YOU.
MY HANDS WANT TO TOUCH YOUR FACE.
MY BODY ACHES FOR YOUR PASSION
AND MY SOUL IS YOURS FOR THE ASKING.
PLEASE CALL ME, PLEASE SEE ME, PLEASE LOVE ME.
PLEASE HOLD ME IN YOUR STRONG ARMS AGAIN.

Kesha august 11.1997

DID I?

THERE IS AN ACHING IN MY HEART
A COLDNESS IN MY SOUL
TEARS FALLING FROM MY EYES
MY MOUTH QUIVERS FROM
CALLING OUT YOUR NAME

IN THE HAUNTING DARKNESS
I REACH OUT TO YOU.
I CALL FOR YOU, I YEARN FOR YOU.
BUT YOU ARE NOT HERE.

SOMETIMES, I MISS YOU SO MUCH I CRY
I HURT SO BADLY
AND IT SEEMS SO LONG
SINCE I HAVE SEEN YOU AT ALL

THEN I HEAR MY OWN SADNESS
ECHO DOWN THE HALL
AND I WONDER:
DID I EVER REALLY KNOW YOU AT ALL?

Kesha 1997

CREEPING/CRAWLING

SLOWLY CREEPING THROUGH THE
DARKNESS OF THE NIGHT
A COLDNESS SO HARSH THAT IS SEEPS
DOWN INTO YOUR VERY BONES.
A SADNESS SO OVER WHELMING,
THAT I WOULD SWEEAR
THAT MY HEART IS BLEEDING.
MEMORIES OF WHAT WAS,
AND DREAMS OF WHAT
COULD HAVE BEEN
START FALLING, FALLING
LIKE ICE CUBES FROM MY SOULS
MIXING WITH THE RAIN FROM ABOVE.
AS YOUR LAUGHTER ECHO'S
THROUGH THIS HOLLOW HOUSE WITH OUT WALLS.

AUGUST 1997/KESHA LAINE.

PATTERNS

THE CHILLY EVENING AIR BRUSHES PAST MY FACE
A SINGLE RAIN DROP GLIDES AND GLISTENS
AND SILENTLY FALLS FROM THE FENCE POST.
THE RUSTY COLORED DARKENED IMPRINTS
OF THE LEAVES CATCH M Y EYE.
AGAINST THE ABANDONED PATIO
I NOTE THE VARIOUS SIZES AND COLORS
OF IMPRINTS FROM THE LEAVES
THAT HAVE BRIEFLY LAIN THERE,
THEN WERE BLOWN AWAY IN THE NIGHT.
SILENTLY LEAVING A MOURNFUL TRAIL BEHIND.

ONE SOULFUL SMALL DARKENED LEAF REMAINS.
BARELY FLUTTERING, THEN STILL AGAIN.
ALL ALONE ON THE COLD HARD CEMENT.
AMID GIANT PATTERNS OF LEAVES GONE ON BEFORE.
I HEAR A FAINT WHISTLE, A MOURNFUL CRY
FROM THE TREE ABOVE.
HER LEAVES, ONCE BRIGHT AND NEW,
AND FULL OF LIFE,
ARE SLOWLY, GRACEFULLY
FADING AND WANING INTO THE AUTUM NIGHT
FRAIL AND WITHERED THEY FALL. ONE, TWO, THREE.
THEY DRIFT AWAY. ALMOST STOLEN IN THEIR PRIME

kesha

THEN SUDDENDLY

ALMOST WITHOUT WARNING:
THE REST OF THE LEAVES BEGIN TO FLUTTER
IN THE BREEZE, DRIFTING HERE AND THERE.

THEN, THEY ARE GONE
A CHILL, ALMOST BRISK WIND BEGINS.
THE ONE SMALL LEAF FLUTTERS, ROLLS
AND DRIFTS ACROSS MY TOES
THEN IS GONE.
AND I AM ALONE IN THE SILENT DARKNESS
AMID TRACES OF LIFE THAT IS NO MORE.

IN THE DISTANCE, I HEAR A SHUFFLE
A CRUNCHING, MUFFLELED SOUND.
OF SOMEONE WALKING
THE SOLES OF THEIR SHOES PRESSING
PATTERENS OF THE NOW DECEASED LIVES.
INTO THE PAVEMENT.
SILENCENING THEIR LONELY CRIES)
FOOT STEPS IN THE NIGHT,
FAST APPROACHING, THEN SLOWLY,
ALMOST HESITANTLY,
THEN HE TOO
IS GONE.

LEAVING ME OUTSIDE IN THE NIGHT.
PEERING INTO THE WINDOW OF MY HOUSE
STANDING ON MY TIPTOES, LOOKING IN
SEARCHING, HOPING,

ALMOST AFRAID TO SEE
IF SOMEONE IS THERE. ALIVE.
SOMEWHERE INSIDE ME, IN MY SOUL,
IS THERE STILL A LIFE?
.. OR
IS MY LIFE STILL?.......

NOVEMBER 97/K

COLD REALITY

THE COLD NOVEMBER NIGHT IS DEEPENING
THE SHADES OF GRAY MIXING WITH THE CLOUDS
STREAKS OF MOON BEAMS APPEAR TO GENTLY
LIGHTEN THE SKY. BRIEFLY, THEN
WANING AND IS GONE.

GONE SO FAST, THAT YOU WONDER
IF IT HAPPENED AT ALL.
THE STILLNESS AND SILENCE ARE DEAFENING.
NO DISTANT ROAR, NO SIGNS OF LIFE NEAR OR FAR.

SO QUIET, THE BEATING OF MY HEART
LIKE AN ECHO, SLOW, LOUD, EVEN
THEN QUICKER AND LOUDER UNTIL
I ALMOST SCREAM FROM THE THUNDEROUS NOISE.

THEN, I AWAKEN. DRENCHED., IN SWEAT
AND CHILLED. SHAKING, AND BREATHLESS
AFRAID, ALONE.
WITHOUT YOU…

NOV. 1997

Fleeting moments gone

I HAVE CLIMBED THE STEEPEST HILLSIDES,
AND WANDERED
THROUGH THE MUDDY, FLOODS.
I HAVE FLOWN ACROSS THE STATES,
BUT, ALAS! I HAVE NOT FOUND TRUE LOVE.

I HAVE SEARCHED FOR IT HIGH AND LOW
I TURNED EVERY CORNER CAREFULLY
AND WATCHED. AND WAITED.
HOPING TO FIND THAT ELLUSIVE FEELING.
BUT, I HAVE ALWAYS LEFT, FEELING UNSAITED.

I WOULD GO TO THE END OF THE EARTH
JUST TO FIND IT.
I WOULD SKYDIVE OR LEARN TO SWIM
I WOULD STAY AWAKE ALL NIGHT.
AND BE AFRAID THAT I WOULD MISS IT

I'VE CAUGHT A GLIMPSE OF IT-ONCE.
IN SOMEONES STEEL BLUE EYES
IN SOMEONES LAUGHTER

I THOUGHT I CAUGHT IT ONCE.
ONCE, SO LONG AGO.
BUT NOW, I FIND MYSELF CHASING
AFTER OTHER THINGS.
THAT REALITY BRINGS.
I'VE LOOKED FOR HOPE
I'VE DREAMED OF MEETING SOMEONE
I COULD TRUST.

I THOUGHT I HAD FELT IT ONCE
IN A MAN I KNEW.
BUT ALL OF THESE FEARS,
KEPT ME AWAY FROM YOU.

I HAVE SPENT YEARS SEARCHING
AND YEARS YEARNING
FOR THAT FEELING OF LOVE.
I HAVE EVEN PRAYED TO
THE HEAVENS ABOVE

I KNOW THERE IS SOMEONE
OUT THERE, WAITING
WISHING
WANTING
JUST LIKE ME.

?1997/KESHA LAINE.

THE FORBIDDEN

IN THE DISTANT SHADOWS
IN THE MIST OF LATE NIGHT
IN THE LIGHT OF THE MOON
AND THE SOUND OF A TRAIN
IN A FOG, I LOOK UP
AND I SEE YOU
WALKING TOWARD ME

THAT WALK
THAT SWAGER
THAT WAY YOU HAVE ABOUT YOU.
THEN I SEE YOUR SMILE
I SEE THE COOL STEELE BLUE EYES
I HEAR THE SOFT HUSKINESS
OF YOUR VOICE
AND THEN,
I FALL

YOU PUT YOUR STRONG ARMS AROUND ME
HUGGING ME SO TIGHT
LIFTING ME UPWARD
AND INWARD
SLOWLY, GENTLY
SOFTLY, SILENTLY
LIFTING ME INTO YOUR HEART.....................

QUSAY-MEANS DISTANT/1998

GRIEF

I LOVED YOU ONCE
IN A DREAM I HAD, LONG AGO
IN A SIMPLER LAND
I REMEMBER JOYFUL LAUGHTER
AND GIGGLES AND I SAW
RAYS OF SUNSHINE
I THOUGHT I HAD FINALLY FOUND
THE LIFE I WAS AFTER.
BUT THE STORMS BEGAN
THE SEASONS GREW LONG
I GREW WEARY OF THE LIFE
OF THE SAD, AND LONELY SONGS
I THOUGHT I KNEW YOU,
IN A DREAM LONG AGO.
BUT I WAS WRONG
AND I TRIED TO LET YOU GO.
BUT THE MEMORY OF YOUR FACE
OCCASSIONALLY CROSSES MY MIND
AND ONCE IN A WHILE
I FIND MYSELF SMILING, CRYING.
AND FINALLY SLEEPING
AND I KNOW FOR NOW
I'LL NO LONGER BE GRIEVING.

Kesha/august 23, 1998

BROKEN WINGS

A BROKEN WING
CAN GROUND A DOVE
A BROKEN WING
CAN CHALLENGE LOVE
THE LESSONS OF LIFE
ARE HARD AND LONG
MANY RIDDLES TO SOLVE
AND ROADS TO TRAVEL ON.
THE PATHS ARE STEEP
AND VERY ROCKY
BUT IF YOU BELIEVE--
IT CAN HAPPEN TO YOU...
THEN, HAVE FAITH, AND HOPE
AND STARE DEFEAT IN THE EYE.
AND WALK ON, WALK PAST
KEEP GOING ON
TIL YOU GET THERE
WHERE YOU WANT TO BE
THEN FLY GIRL, FLY
FLY HIGH, AND BE FREE

kesha

STILLNESS

IN THE LATE NIGHT SHADOWS
I HEAR YOUR VOICE
FAINT AND DISTANT
BUT TRUE AND CLEAR
THROUGH THE MIST
IN THE DARK SKY,
THE CLOUDLESS SKY
I SEE THE SADNESS
IN THE MOONLIGHT
GLIMMER, FAINTLY
THEN, I SEE
THE FIRST RAYS OF HOPE
IF I LET YOU IN MY HEART
AS THE NIGHT WEARS ON,
CLOSER AND CLOSSER TO DAWN
I FEEL THE WARMTH OF
YOUR EMBRACE.
AS I DREAM OF HOLDING YOU
I SEE THE SMILE ON YOUR FACE.

AS THE SKY BURNS BRIGHTER
AND THE SUN BEGINS TO RISE
AS IT PEEPS ABOVE THE HILLSIDE
I START TO BELIEVE IN SOMETHING
IT SEEMS LIKE A MILLION YEARS
AND MY HEART BEGINS TO ACHE
AS I START TO FALL FOR YOU
AND I TREMBLE AS I
START TO LOVE YOU TOO.
Kesha

CHARMER

YOU CHARMED YOUR WAY INTO MY LIFE
NEITHER ONE OF US WAS AWARE OF IT
BUT YOUR SMILE AND YOU LAUGH
INCHED ITS WAY INTO MY HEART.
IT FOUND A WAY INTO MY SOUL
NOW MY SMILE AND MY LAUGH
ARE A REFLECTION OF YOUR LOVE
GIVEN TO ME EFFORTLESSLY
UNKNOWING AND UNSELFISHLY
IT WAS SO SILENT, CREEPING INTO ME
THAT I HARDLY KNEW WHAT WAS HAPPENING.
AFTER ALL THE PRIOR STRUGGLES
THE PAIN, THE LONLINESS
I CAN FINALLY SMILE,
AND LAUGH,
AND NOW, MY TEARS ARE
TEARS OF JOY.

OF WHAT MISERY I HAVE KNOWN
LOOKING FOR SOMETHING, SOMEONE
I THOUGHT I WOULD NEVER FIND.
BUT CREEPING AROUND THE CORNER
PAST THE IMAGINARY WALL
CAME THIS BOLDER,
THIS GENTLY ROLLING BALL
OF LOVE,
MELTING MY HEART
SOOTHING MY MIND
AND LOVING ME

kesha

TO HIM

THERE IS STRENGTH I FEEL IN YOUR WARM EMBRACE
THERE IS A QUIET CALM I FEEL
WHEN YOU ARE NEAR ME.
YOUR HAND REACHES OUT
YOUR FACE TURNS TOWARD ME
YOUR ARMS OUTSTRETCHED
REACHING, JUST FOR ME.
THEN YOU HOLD ME. YOU TOUCH MY FACE.
AND KISS MY LIPS. SLOWLY,
MELTING MY ONCE FROZEN HEART.
I CAN HARDLY BELIEVE IT!
ONCE IT WAS JUST A DREAM.
BUT NOW, YOU ARE REALLY HERE.
JUST HERE, WITH ME.
AND OF COURSE, YOU PROMISE
TO NEVER LEAVE.
BUT TO MY FEAR, AS PROVEN MANY TIMES BEFORE.
I AM LEARY, AND SKEPTICAL,
BUT YOU ARE STILL HERE. MONTH AFTER MONTH.

YEAR AFTER YEAR.
YOU HAVENT LEFT ME.
YOU STILL KISS ME SOFTLY.
YOU STILL REACH OUT FOR ME
YOU ARE STILL HERE,
AFTER ALL THESE YEARS.
AND I AM STILL AMAZED
THAT YOU, YOU LOVE ME STILL.

kesha

THE ENTIRE MANUSCRIPT HAS BEEN WRITTEN
BY ME, WITHOUT ANY CO-WRITERS.
I OWN ALL OF THIS WORK. I HAVE BEEN
WRITING POETRY SINCE I WAS 13 YEARS OLD.

Printed in the United States
By Bookmasters